Bouncy
and
The Power of Yet

Jim "🏀" Jones

Brenda Jones

This book is dedicated to our parents - Donna, Dale, Bonnie and Bernard. They instilled in us the belief we can always learn and not to be afraid to make mistakes. We have tried to pass this same wisdom down to our children.

BOUNCY AND THE POWER OF YET
Copyright © 2020 by Jim and Brenda Jones
Published by Jim Jones Enterprises LLC, Avon Lake, OH

All rights reserved. Printed in the United States of America. No part of this book may be used or reproduced in any manner whatsoever without written permission except in the case of brief quotations embodied in critical articles or reviews. This book is a work of fiction. Names, characters, businesses, organizations, places, events and incidents either are the product of the author's imagination or are used fictitiously. Any resemblance to actual persons, living or dead, events, or locales is entirely coincidental.

For information regarding permissions email: JimBballJones@gmail.com or visit JimBasketballJones.com

Paperback ISBN: 978-1-7350356-4-2
Hard cover ISBN: 978-1-7350356-5-9

First Edition: January 2021

Bouncy

and
The Power of Yet

Jim and Brenda Jones

Bouncy the Basketball woke with a start. "What was that?!!"

He heard whimpering from a remote-control car sitting in the corner.

Bouncy rolled off his shelf and did a belly flop onto the floor.

(Bouncy was a basketball who couldn't bounce, but that's another story.)

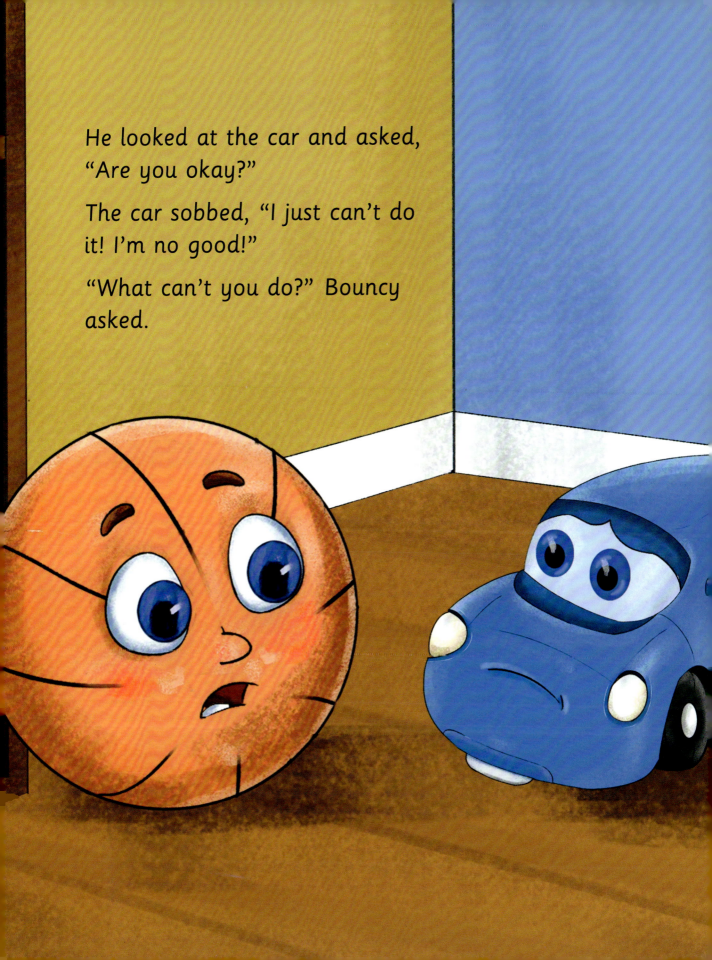

He looked at the car and asked, "Are you okay?"

The car sobbed, "I just can't do it! I'm no good!"

"What can't you do?" Bouncy asked.

The car looked up at Bouncy. "I can't jump the ramp. My box said I jump ramps, but I'm too scared! What if I crash? What if my wheels come off and everybody laughs at me?!!"

Bouncy remembered how sad he felt the first time he couldn't bounce. He asked, "What's your name?"

A big tear ran down the car's windshield. **"Speedy."**

Bouncy nodded. "It's going to be okay, Speedy. You can learn to jump!"

Speedy dried his tears with his windshield wipers. "Really?"

Bouncy wiggled, nodded yes and said, "I'll take you to Yeti! He knows The Power of Yet!"

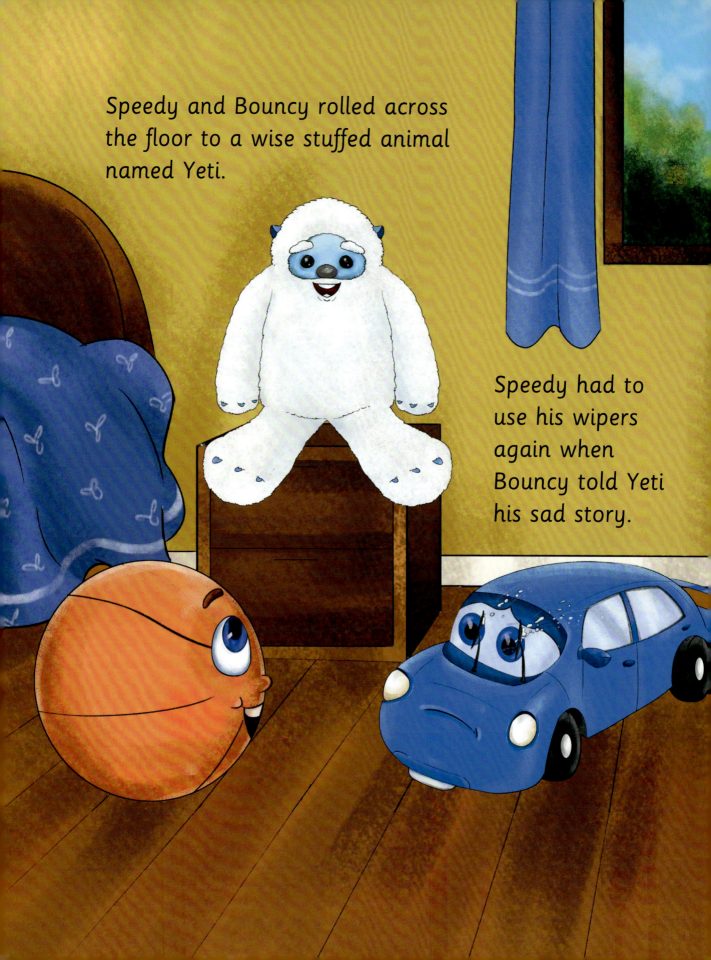

Speedy and Bouncy rolled across the floor to a wise stuffed animal named Yeti.

Speedy had to use his wipers again when Bouncy told Yeti his sad story.

Yeti smiled. "I know all about feeling scared. Cal's mom bought me to help Cal when he has a hard time or is afraid he'll fail."

He looked at Speedy. "Show us what you can do!"

Speedy sped around the floor. He did wheelies and beeped his horn.

Yeti clapped and Bouncy yelled, "Go, Speedy, go!"

As Speedy came to the ramp he zoomed off to the side. No way was he going over that ramp. It was too tall and scary!

"Now we know why they call you Speedy!" Yeti said.

Speedy came to a stop in front of Yeti. He said softly, "I can go super-fast, but I'm afraid of the ramp."

Bouncy asked Speedy, "What if we start with something really easy and then we'll make it a little harder as we go. Will you try?"

Speedy shrugged. "I guess so."

"Good Speedy." Yeti said. "Now, it's okay to crash. It's okay to fail. We won't laugh at you. You don't know how to jump the ramp, yet. We'll help you learn."

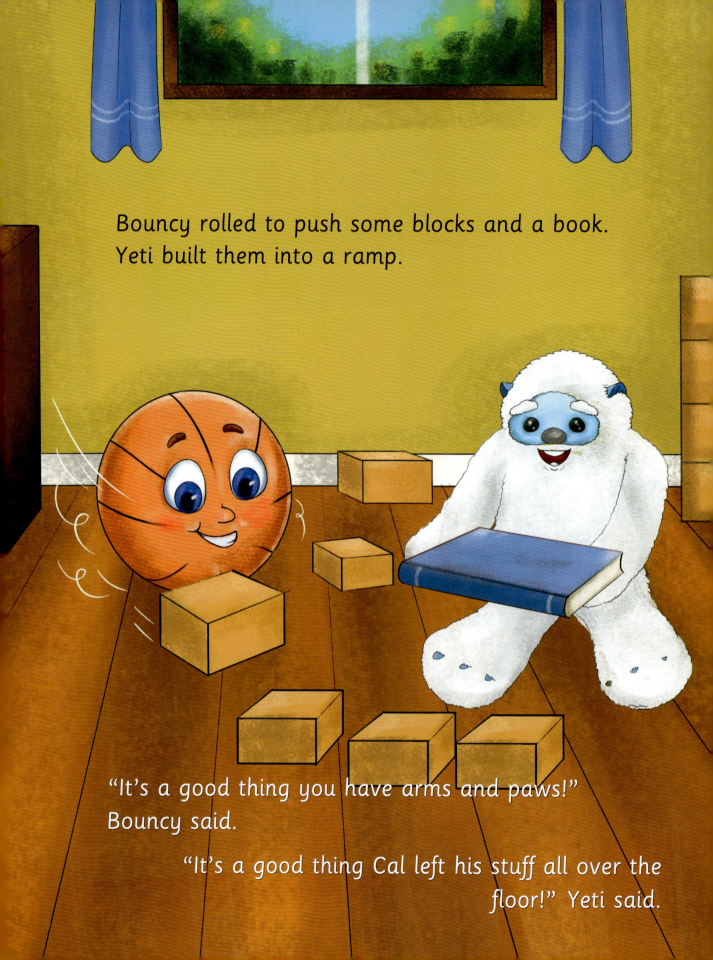

Bouncy rolled to push some blocks and a book.
Yeti built them into a ramp.

"It's a good thing you have arms and paws!" Bouncy said.

"It's a good thing Cal left his stuff all over the floor!" Yeti said.

Bouncy told Speedy, "Close your eyes and pretend you're going over this little ramp."

Speedy closed his eyes. "I see myself flying, just a little."

Yeti said, "That's right, Speedy. Now, open your eyes and try it."

Speedy took a deep breath and started his engine. He drove over the small ramp and landed with a little bump.

"Wow! I did it! That wasn't too hard!"

Bouncy said, "Great job, Speedy! Let's make it a bit taller."

Bouncy pushed more blocks and then he asked, "Is this enough?"

Yeti said, "Yep! We don't want to build it very tall... YET!"

Speedy sailed over the new ramp and landed with a big thump!

He shouted, "I did it! It's getting easier!"

Yeti said, "Good! It's time for the plastic ramp!" He dragged the big ramp to the middle of the room.

Yeti put a paw on Speedy.

"You don't have to be great to try, but if you don't try you'll never be great."

Speedy took a deep breath and slowly let it out.

This ramp really wasn't much taller than the other one. Hitting the gas pedal, he sped toward the ramp.

Eeek! He shut his eyes tight!

Suddenly, he was flying through the air and...

CRASH!

He landed in a pile of Cal's stinky socks.

"Hooray!"

Bouncy and Yeti cheered. "You did it!"

Speedy smiled big. "Did you see me? I went over the ramp!"

Bouncy said, "You sure did, Speedy! Next time maybe keep your eyes open."

Speedy drove to the starting line, revved his engine and kept his eyes wide open. He raced towards the ramp, flew through the air and landed safely on the floor.

"Wahoo!" Bouncy whooped.

"Yay!" Yeti yelled.

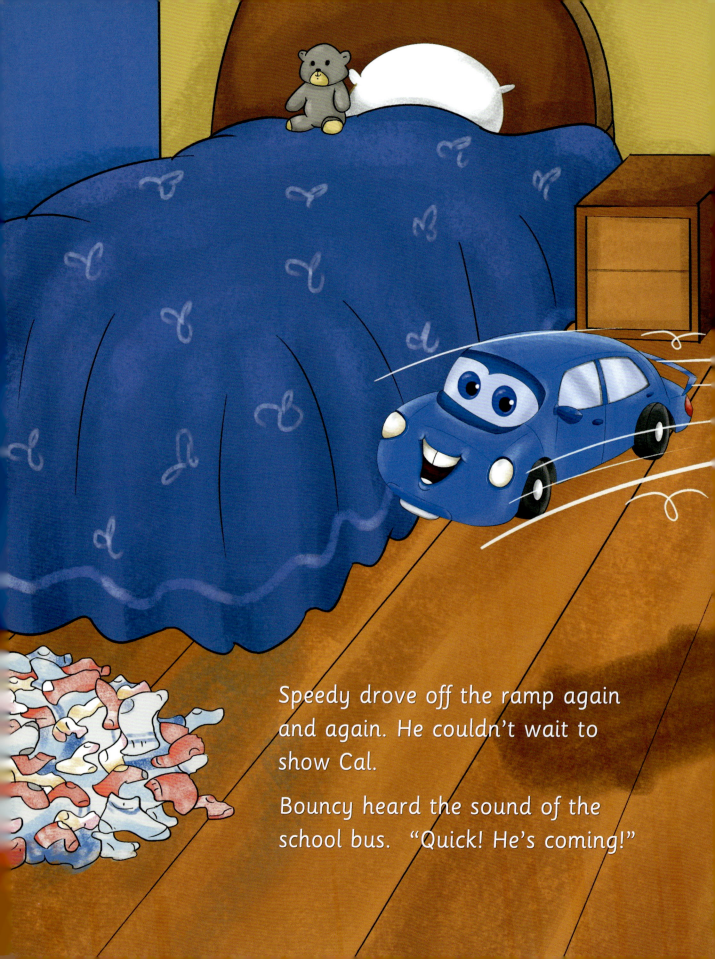

Speedy drove off the ramp again and again. He couldn't wait to show Cal.

Bouncy heard the sound of the school bus. "Quick! He's coming!"

As Cal opened the door to his room, Speedy raced up the ramp, flew through the air and made a perfect landing.

Cal yelled,

"Speedy! You did it!"

"It's fun!" Speedy said. "I just hadn't done it, yet!"

Yeti said, "Remember, to learn something new, keep trying…"

Bouncy, Speedy and Cal yelled,

"You just don't know it, YET!!!"

Bouncy and Friends Book Series

All books available at www.JimBasketballJones.com/shop

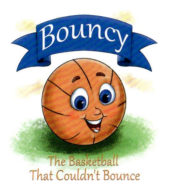

The first book in the series is *Bouncy: The Basketball That Couldn't Bounce*. Bouncy is an adorable and lovable basketball that feels hopeless and sad when he finds out he can't bounce. A boy named Cal finds Bouncy and says to him, "You are the one and only you. I'll help you find what you can do."

This picture book helps children realize that they are unique and special.

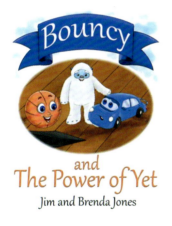

In the second book, Bouncy and The Power of Yet, Bouncy and Yeti help a remote control car, Speedy, overcome his fears about jumping over a ramp. "My box said I jump ramps, but I'm too scared! What if I crash? What if my wheels come off and everybody laughs at me?!!" Speedy explains. Yeti helps Speedy realize he just doesn't know how to jump the ramp YET, but he can learn.

This picture book helps children realize they can learn new things and it's okay to make mistakes. You just don't know it yet. You can get your own Yeti stuffed animal at:

www.JimBasketballJones.com/shop.

In the third book in the series, Bouncy and Cal's Big Show, Cal and Bouncy are struggling to create a fun basketball routine for the school Talent Show. Cal's mom gives them a secret tip that makes learning the new routine a "piece of cake." It works, but then the night of the BIG SHOW they lose the piece of cake. Speedy and Yeti have to come to the rescue and get the piece of cake to the school before the Talent Show.

In this fun and adventuresome picture book children discover a secret tip on how to make learning a "piece of cake."

About the Authors

Jim "Basketball" Jones is a National Youth Motivational Speaker and Author with over 20 years as a professional school assembly speaker. With over 8,000 school assemblies performed, Jim is a leader in the school assembly and character education field.

Book Jim for an **Author Visit** or **School Assembly** for your school. Find out how to schedule Jim at: www.JimBasketballJones.com. You can follow Jim on Facebook @JimBasketballJones and Twitter @JimBballJones

Brenda Jones, M. Ed, is an award winning educator (Franklin B Walters Award Recipient) with over 25 years of teaching experience. She loves using her Yeti to inspire her students to keep trying. On a daily basis she will remind her students, "You just don't know it, YET! You can follow her on Twitter @KdngDisneyJones